M000266026

Alejandra
First Lady of the New
Bent's Old Fort

Alejandra
First Lady of the New
 Bent's Old Fort

Alejandra A. Aldred-Adams

East of the Mountains and West of the Sun™
RHYOLITE PRESS LLC
Colorado Springs, Colorado

Alejandra - First Lady of the New Bent's Old Fort

Aldred-Adams, Alejandra A.

First Edition   Mar 8, 2021

ISBN: 978-1-943829-33-0

Library of Congress Control No. 2021904696

Published in the United States of America by
Rhyolite Press, LLC
P.O. Box 60144
Colorado Springs, Colorado 80960

www.rhyolitepress.com

Painting on front cover by Carrie Arnold
Editorial & Facilitation: Ed and Clara Lee Stafford
Book design & layout by Susie Schorsch
Cover design by Donald Kallaus

PRINTED AND BOUND IN THE UNITED STATES OF AMERICA

This book is dedicated to my parents, Hilario and Juanita Gonzales, without whom there would not have been an Alejandra.

Also, to my husband Delbert Warren Aldred, my hero, who believed in me and gave me the courage to persevere, no matter the obstacles I might encounter in life. He was "the wind beneath my wings."

And, to my beloved sister Guadalupe Herrera, my rock and confidant.

A special dedication to my best and dear friend
Kathryn R. Wise for sponsoring *Alejandra First
Lady of the New Bent's Old Fort*; and also for her
ongoing support and encouragement to see the
finished project.

Acknowledgments

I am deeply indebted to Marsha Hall, retired elementary and Middle school teacher in Commerce City, Colorado, for suggesting that I write about the legacy of the fort "through my eyes."

I am indebted, also, to the Rev. Dr. Alphonsus Ihuoma, my son, who helped me prepare my notes and photos. Also, he encouraged me to pursue this book.

To Ed and Clara Lee Stafford, who so wonderfully took on the task of editing and helping me with their patience and positive prodding. In the spring of 1991, I had the privilege of cooking and serving a meal in the fort dining room for Ed Stafford and others. At the time, little did I know, he would be the one to help me with my book. Ed and his wife Clara Lee have been a great inspiration to me. They have worked tirelessly in their commitment to see this project come to fruition.

Also, Thank you, Barbara Van Cleve for the use of your beautiful black and white photographs.

Fort blacksmith George Ainsle and Alejandra's husband Dell Aldred, facing horses, are giving a demonstration to Winter Quarters participants on hitching a team to a wagon.
Photograph by Barbara Van Cleve©1983.

Photographs in this book are from the author's photo collection, unless otherwise stated and are used with permission.

Book Cover: Painting of Bent's Old Fort with Alejandra Aldred-Adams standing in front of the northeast bastion. Painting by Carrie Arnold. Artist Carrie and her husband, Sam, based their adobe restaurant (The Fort) in Morrison, Colorado, on a drawing they saw of Bent's Old Fort. They were supporters and attended events over the years at Bent's Fort. The painting on the cover is hanging in Alejandra's living room.

Contents

Preface

It occurred to me, after doing the math, that I was the only full-time employee at Bent's Old Fort, National Historic Site (NHS) who had been an eyewitness to the rebirth of Mr. Bent's "mud castle" from an archaeological excavation to its reconstruction by the National Park Service.

The life of the original trading fort was 16 years (1833 to 1849). My tenure at the fort was 27 years. I had outlived the original fort!

On June 10, 1979, a signing was held at the reconstructed fort by authors who had written the book *Bent's Old Fort NHS* for publication by the State Historical Society of Colorado. It included an episodic history of the fort from its 19th century beginning through its rebirth in the 1970s. My copy of the book was autographed by all five of the authors.

Following are two of these authors' inscriptions in my copy:

Alex—first lady of the new Bent's Old Fort, with affection. — Enid T. Thompson, 6-10-1979

To my favorite gal who runs the fort. — George A. Thorson, 6-10-1979

After some thought, I considered Enid Thompson's inscription and found it absolutely correct. I was the first lady of the newly re-constructed fort because I was there at the beginning of the recon-struction until I retired. The last 16 years of my time at Bent's Fort were the reconstructed fort's first 16 years. I had been working for the historic site from 1968 to 1995.

I had seen it all.

After being retired for several years, some friends requested I give a tour to them and some out-of-town family guests. When we were finished, they said, "We have visited the fort many times and have never received the informative and interactive tour." Another group of elementary school teachers from Denver (including my sister) requested a guided tour since they had never been to the fort. One of their number encouraged me to write a book about my time at Bent's Old Fort.

Although those who encouraged me to write this book did so be-cause they liked my informative tours, I had another greater reason. One major thing I learned while studying Bent's Fort was laboring women had no voice. At least in one way, by portraying a Mexican woman from that time as an interpreter at the fort, I gave them a voice. I made the many visitors to the fort aware that these women, like many women of their time, were an important part of history.

Mexican laborers hired by Bent, St. Vrain and Company to work in and around the fort made up a vast majority of the residents. Their work was extremely hard, certainly essential, and their status unimaginably low. Mexican laboring women were valued even less. It is for this reason that their story has not been told, not the way that I wished for it to be told.

I wanted to share my personal experiences as a "living history" medium, as a Mexican laborer woman in the reconstructed fort, with all the tools provided to recreate my role. I wanted to provide a focal point for diverse cultural interaction. My story would bring together the Mexican laborer woman with other character roles, insofar as such interaction would have occurred.

I wanted to give a vivid picture of the actual activities the Mexican laborer woman performed using the hands-on concept, not only inside the fort but outside the fort walls, as well. I wanted the visitor to the fort to participate in the life of the women who worked at Bent's Fort.

Today I want to document the 20th century point of view of a Hispanic woman's lifestyle doing the same activities that a 19th century Mexican laborer woman performed using the same tools.

Overall, this book should be a source of information for future generations to give a perspective of the Mexican laborer woman's role at the fort.

First winter after the reconstructed Bent's Old Fort.

From Ruins to Reconstruction

It was a privilege to witness the reconstruction of Bent's Old Fort from start to finish. The project was started in 1975, and a year later was completed. It coincided with Colorado State's Centennial and the Nation's Bicentennial. Although much is written about the history of the fort, the valiant effort that was made by the Daughters of the American Revolution (DAR) and local community to save the history of the location must be remembered, too. Also, the efforts that went into recreating the fort should be lauded. Volunteers and staff members who have worked at the recreated fort must also be recognized for the work they do to keep the history alive.

For sixteen years (1833–1849), Bent, St. Vrain and Company had a prosperous trading empire, which included the fur trade, Indian trade, and Mexican trade. The fort was at its highest peak, both commercially and politically, during these years. The reconstruction of the fort replicated the years 1845–46.

Lt. James W. Abert, a U. S. Topographical Engineer convalescing at the fort in 1846, measured and sketched the fort, which provided the only existing drawings of the original structure.

George Thorson was director of design and project manager for the reconstruction of Bent's Old Fort. In his article "The Architectural Challenges" he pointed out the difficulties of even beginning the reconstruction of Bent's Old Fort.

Besides its historical significance, the fort was architecturally unique; it represented the first major adobe structure of the Southwest designed by and for Anglos. With its corner bastions providing lookout firing positions along the walled enclosure, it was entitled to be called a fort, and its impressive facade had a military air about it. However, its interior was designed primarily to serve its major function—trade. The style and the construction techniques were basically Spanish Colonial, but the function of the fort was to serve the American commercial enterprise.

The architects were interested in all of the details regarding the structure and the life styles that would shed light on the fort's uses. No company records survived, but there were written descriptions by at least twenty-five primary eyewitnesses, a surprisingly large number considering the prevailing illiteracy of the period. These statements gave clues to the general appearance of the fort, the facilities and their use, and sometimes actual dimensions or materials. As expected, the data was far from complete and puzzles abounded. Bent's Old Fort was built 'by guess and by God,' by experienced amateurs. There was no architect nor engineer to provide posterity with "as built" drawings and specifications. There were, of course, no photographs.

Initially, the reconstructed fort was furnished with both antiques and reproductions of the period. Some of the rooms had barriers, such as small iron chains strung across doorways or wood gates. Waist-high barriers were also installed to protect the antique furnishings. Eventually, the antiques were replaced with reproductions and most barriers were removed.

As an authentic reconstructed fort, the National Park Service

Reproduction of trade room at Bent's Fort.

had a vision to use the fort as a "living history" medium. The "living history" program would bring the fort alive, using permanent and seasonal staff and volunteers attired in clothing of the period. The concept would give an opportunity for the public to interact with employees portraying characters of the period and possibly get a "hands-on" experience of life in a fur trading post.

For a period of twenty years, 1975 to 1995, I portrayed the character of a Mexican laborer woman, telling the story to the visiting public in what I hoped was a compelling manner. The story of Mexican laborer women is one of the least documented in primary sources, insofar as explicitly giving detailed description of the activities and lifestyle. The Mexican laborers made a major contribution in building and maintaining the fort and caring for the livestock.

Although Mexican laborers were an integral part of life at Bent's Fort, they were not recognized as such by eyewitnesses, being worth noting due to their social status. Mexican laborers were the work horses of the fort. Their labor was cheap. They were paid five to ten dollars a month, and much of it was paid in trade goods such as coffee, sugar, bolts of material (red flannel or calico), beans, and other materials, all marked up more than their worth.

My character as a Mexican laborer woman was more than dressing up and portraying a character. It was about giving the flavor of who I was, displaying involvement, demonstrating, empowering, and giving a "hands-on" experience. I also needed to be sufficiently well read to answer questions about other living history characters, such as the blacksmith, cook, or trappers.

Visitors departed the fort wanting to know more about Bent's Old Fort and its importance to the opening of the American West. The National Park Service instilled in all visitors the fact that the fort belongs to them, and we are entrusted to protect and preserve the resource for future generations.

Reproductions give that authetic feel to the fort.

Alejandra's portrayal of a Mexican laborer.
Photograph by Barbara Van Cleve©1983

First Impressions

Sometime in the fall of 1968, the clerk typing position became vacant at Bent's Old Fort National Historic Site. I applied for the position and was selected. I was hired by Park Superintendent William Featherstone. My starting date was December 16, 1968.

The duties consisted of providing clerical and typing services for the superintendent, plus being the office receptionist, meeting and informing park visitors about points of interest in the park.

Bent's Old Fort NHS had been established on March 15, 1963, as part of the National Park Service. Prior to my arrival, the Park Service had conducted a thorough archaeological investigation (1963–1966) of the site to determine the layout and actual size of the fort. Thousands of artifacts were uncovered, collected, and cataloged for future reference. The site was a little over a quarter of a mile from a trailer house converted to an office.

In 1968, the fort ruins were in different stages of deterioration. Some of the original walls were capped with a mixture of cement preservative to keep the walls from further deteriorating. Other areas, below-ground room and a cistern, were covered with plywood shelters. In the center of the plaza was the reproduction of the fort's fur press, although with further research, documentation showed the fur press to be a screw-type press. A fur press was standard equipment at a trading company and compressed fur pelts so that they could be baled for easier travel.

Upon arrival at the site of the fort ruins, I was in awe. My first impression was this: How did those freight wagons come through the main gate. The gates were not wide. All the rooms were laid out in a cohesive order around the plaza. It looked like a perfect square. I thought to myself, the people who lived here were midgets, based on the size of the quarters. The warehouse seemed larger than the living quarters; living conditions would be harsh in such small quarters. The largest room was the dining room.

PLAZA OF FORT RUINS
Park Technician Alexandra Aldred stands in the plaza of Bent's Old Fort ruins. Ninth anniversary of the creation of Bent's Old Fort National Historic Site of the National Park Service will be observed Wednesday, March 15.

Park technician Alejandra Aldred stands in the plaza of Bent's Old Fort ruins after excavation was completed.
Photo from the *La Junta Tribune-Democrat*.

As I stood there in the middle of the bare ground where once the fort had stood, facing toward the Spanish Peaks to the southwest,

I imagined the Mexican laborers coming toward me wearing rugged clothing, straw sombreros, their shoulders wrapped with Rio Grande blankets, and with leather-soled moccasins on their feet. The women would be wearing *rebozos* over their heads and shoulders as shawls. They would be dressed in red flannel skirts with a full-length flannel chemise and leather-soled slippers.

Left: Entrance to the reconstructed Bent's Old Fort.

Below: View of the central courtyard of the fort showing the fur press.

Most traveled by foot beside *carretas* loaded with water barrels, and gourds filled with drinking water hung along the sides of the *carretas*. Burros would carry all their personal belongings. These Mexican laborers came to the United States from Mexico with the intention of working hard for the Bent, St.Vrain and Company, just like my grandfather's intention was to work hard for the Santa Fe Railroad.

As a Hispanic woman, I was being drawn in by those women who had been at the fort before me. I didn't know at the time that the fort would give me the opportunity to tell their story.

Reconstructed fort taken in the fall of 1977.

Orientation to the Park History

In January 1968, Park Superintendent William Featherstone retired, and historian Robert Davidson was designated Park Superintendent through May 1970. Superintendent Davidson guided me as I learned how to acquire needed information, such as evaluating resources, both primary and secondary. In other words, he taught me about the nuts and bolts and how to use them regarding the fort's history. He was an excellent teacher to have had as I started my Bent's Fort career.

As part of my initial orientation, under the supervision of Mr. Davidson, he identified the first public physical recognition of the site as a granite monument erected in 1912 by A. E. Reynolds, jointly with the Daughters of the American Revolution. The DAR was placing monuments along the Santa Fe Trail. Reynolds felt that the site should be considered for a park.

According to the article, From Ruin to Reconstruction, 1920-1976 by Merrill J. Mattes:

> At the October meeting of the DAR Chapter, A.E. Reynolds and George Williams were present to 'talk over improvements' at the site . . . On 11 November 1920 at a special meeting held

at the home of Judge and Mrs. M.F. Miller, the fort site and access strip 'was given [to] the chapter by Mr. Reynolds and Mr. Williams,' according to the La Junta Chapter records. The 1920 *gift* of the fort site and access strip may have been a verbal promise rather than a legal document. Neither Reynolds nor his foreman Williams owned the land as individuals for on 10 January 1920 the Bent's Fort Land and Cattle Company had been incorporated, with President B.P. Morse, Secretary J.P.M. Humphrey, and principal stockholder A.E. Reynolds as signers. The transaction was not legalized until five years after Reynolds' death in March 1921.

The Santa Fe Trail organization's website gives insight on Albert (A.E.) Reynolds. Born in 1840, he followed the family business as a merchant and by 1865 he and his brother headed west. In 1867, A.E. was awarded the position of Sutler at Old Fort Lyon near the site of Bent's New Fort. A sutler was a merchant that followed the military as their supplier of goods. When New Fort Lyon was constructed in 1868, Mr. Reynolds was appointed there as well. He also engaged in trade with the Cheyenne and Arapaho Indians, and over many years bought land in the Arkansas River Valley which included the site of Bent's Old Fort.

In 1926, the local chapter of the DAR acquired the site of the fort from Reynold's daughter. Also, in 1930 the DAR erected a large rock gate as an entrance to the area located on U.S. Highway 194. In addition, the granite stone marker that was erected by the DAR in 1912 was moved to that entrance gate.

In 1954, the DAR donated the site to the Colorado State Historical Society. The first building to be erected by Bent's Old Fort NHS was a maintenance shop and storage building. From there started the incredible story of the fort's reconstruction. I credit Superintendent Davidson for sharing all of this information, as it became handy for answering visitors' questions.

The title of Park Superintendent was changed to Park Manager when John Patterson was transferred to the site in 1970, replacing Mr. Davidson. Mr. Patterson is credited with having contributed a replica blacksmith shop on the site. It was not built within the fort ruins, but southwest of the present southwest bastion. This blacksmith shop was furnished with a forge, bellows, anvil, vise, and all other shop furnishings. Mr. Patterson worked in the shop producing replica nails, fire steels, hinges, door latches, and other useful objects. It was the most visited area.

Prior to the reconstruction of the fort by the National Park Service in 1975-76, I had a change of title and my first promotion. Along with promotion came wearing a woman's new uniform. I was now not only in administration but took on the role as interpreter.

Blacksmith's shop inside of the reconstructed Bent's Old Fort.

Dual Roles: Administrator and Interpreter

Within a year, in December 1970, I was promoted to a Park Technician position, giving me the dual role of administrator and interpreter. I served as the first-point-of-information contact for visitors. I conducted tours of the fort ruins and performed a variety of technical and clerical duties in business administration.

With the promotion and change in title, I was attired in the women's new park uniform. Wearing a uniform of any type makes the wearer a figure of some authority, so people felt comfortable approaching me for information. I give credit to the donning of the National Park Service uniform for being a turning point in my career, for I love people, and I love to talk.

In 1973, I was promoted to the position of Administrative Clerk, while hoping to be switched to the interpretive division for upward mobility. The position provided administrative service support for operations at the fort. I served as Chief Assistant to the Park Manager on administrative matters and formulated the budget for the park. I also served as acting Park Manager in his absence, functioning with full responsibility in delegating authority. This was a position I held through May of 1978.

In May 1978, my position title was elevated from Park Technician to Supervisory Park Technician. As a front-line supervisor, I was to take training and receive certification. I was immediately enrolled for the next class titled "Interpretive Operations for First-Line Supervisors" conducted at the Stephen T. Mather Training Center, Harpers Ferry, West Virginia.

New Park Service Uniform for Alejandra
Photo courtesy of *La Junta Tribune-Democrat*

History of Bent's Old Fort

Between 1970 and 1975 I did extensive research to better educate myself with the National Park Service goal which was to use the reconstructed fort as a "living history" medium with "hands-on" activities, in order to enhance the visitors' experiences. It is important to know the actual history of the fort: what experiences did the people living at the fort have on a daily basis and how could people today have the same types of experiences?

The original fort was a private enterprise owned by brothers Charles and William Bent and Ceran St. Vrain. William Bent employed approximately 100 Mexican laborers from Northern New Mexico to build a massive structure made of on-site mud in "the middle of nowhere" for the purpose of trading. It was never a military fort. Located on the Santa Fe Trail along the Arkansas River, and on boundary between the United States and Mexico at that time, in its day it played an integral part in the U.S. expansion into the Southwest.

When studying the history of Bent's Fort, Mexicans were often referred to as peons, the term for unskilled laborers of low rank. Bent, St. Vrain and Company brought Mexicans to build the fort knowing their ability to build with adobe bricks. Adobe kept the summer heat out and the winter warmth in. Mexicans had the knowledge and ability to build, but they were not considered important in society. I found this ironic.

There were three types of trading activities at the fort: goods coming from the east to the fort, goods going to Mexico from the fort, and local trade with the Native American tribes in the area.

First, trade goods of American manufacture were hauled, initially by wagons pulled by oxen and later by mules, along the Mountain Branch of the Santa Fe trail from Independence, Missouri. Bent's Fort was roughly halfway between the points of origin of goods to sell and Santa Fe. Some of the goods were left at the fort, and the rest continued down the trail into Mexican territory, where the goods were transferred for trade by St. Vrain and Charles Bent in mercantile outlets in Taos and Santa Fe.

Enid Thompson, in her article "Life in an Adobe Castle 1833-1849" featured in *Colorado Magazine* on Old Bent's Fort, referenced that in the 1830s Mexican gold and silver were highly needed in the United States. The *St. Louis Beacon* wrote the supply of Mexican gold and silver was the guarantee to the continued commercial prosperity of St. Louis. Trade from St. Louis to Santa Fe was a million-dollar-a-year business by the 1840s. Remember this was before the California and Colorado gold rushes.

The second source of trading was goods from Mexico brought in from Santa Fe or Taos to be transported east. Some would remain at the fort while the rest went on to Missouri.

Finally, the third source of trading was locally with tribes passing through Bent's Fort, including Southern Cheyenne, Arapaho, Ute, Northern Apache, Kiowa, and Comanche. These tribes either traded their tanned buffalo robes for manufactured goods at the fort or with fort-employed traders traveling to the Indian camps. They traded for factory-made items from St. Louis, such as beads, tobacco, knives, iron kettles, bolts of cloth, clay pipes, small mirrors, blankets, and vermilion.

The trading season was during the winter, the time of year

when the buffalo robe was at its prime. Also, the tribes had already removed fresh flesh and tanned the hides with the fresh brains and liver of the buffalo to cure them for trade.

In 1837, William Bent married Owl Woman, the daughter of Gray Thunder, a Cheyenne Chief and Keeper of the Medicine Arrows. The marriage strengthened ties with the Cheyenne Indians and allowed Owl Woman to visit the fort. The marriage benefited William Bent in trading with the tribes. The fort also relied heavily on family members to maintain the business. William and Charles' brothers, George and Robert, along with Marcellin St. Vrain helped the enterprise work smoothly.

In order to prepare myself about the history of the fort, I read David Lavender's history *Bent's Fort*. A review by Amron Gravett on the Library Thing website (librarything.com) stated what I was aware of: Native Americans were held in higher esteem than Mexican workers. The review stated the following:

> For a book written in 1954, "Bent's Fort" is surprisingly just in its treatment of Native Americans—this was, after all, at a time when John Chivington was still a heroic Indian fighter rather than the perpetrator of a massacre. Although Lavender sometimes calls the Plains tribes "savages", he also notes they were treated extremely poorly by the US government and by most traders. The Bents were also uncharacteristically fair in their treatment of natives—for the time. The Bent brothers built their fort in Cheyenne territory, and William married the Cheyenne chief White Thunder's daughter, Owl Woman, and after her death, her sister, Yellow Woman; the Bents always tried to look after the interests of the Cheyenne.

Mexican Quarters and Mexican Labor

When the fort was reconstructed by the National Park Service, it had been placed on the "footprint" of the original fort, following the floor plan drawn by cartographer Lt. James Abert of General Stephen Kearny's Army of the West in 1846. Looking at photographs of the fort, the Mexican laborers' quarters were to the right of the fort's entry. The turrets or bastions were located in the northeast and southwest corners. The corral was on the opposite side of the entry behind the square open plaza at the center.

It was in the rooms where the Mexican laborers lived during their stay at Bent's Fort that I worked as an interpreter. The rooms were entered from the plaza. They had two windows, one vertical and the other horizontal. Both windows have slats and shutters. The slats are for keeping the chickens from flying into the room. Sometimes the chickens came in the entrance door and ate corn on display there. They were almost tame, so it was easy to shoo them out. The shutters were closed for privacy or for warmth in the winter months.

The three rooms used for living quarters each had a corner fireplace. Each fireplace was quite small but served the intended purposes—cooking and warmth. Lighting for the rooms was hand-dipped candles using buffalo tallow, which is the fat surrounding the large stomach of the buffalo. The tallow was rendered in a cast iron kettle, and after rendering, all the debris was removed and cooled somewhat. The candle wick was dipped and drawn up through the tallow until it was fat enough to form a candle, one of the many jobs for the Mexican laborers.

Door leading to the Mexican Quarters is shown at right. The cooking fire was in front of the Quarters.

The rooms were sparsely furnished. Can you imagine ten people sleeping in one of these small rooms? Individuals used buffalo robes for bedding with straw for mattresses. During the day, the robes were rolled up and used as seating with the backs of the laborers leaning against the walls. Rio Grande blankets were used for warmth and also used as pillows.

Rio Grande blankets could be found at Bent's Fort; they date back to the arrival of the Spaniards in North America in the late 1500s and were used by the common person at the time as they were inexpensive, simple in design, loose-woven blankets.

Alejandra wears her pancho
made from a Rio Grande
style-blanket.

The interior of two
different rooms in the
reconstructed Mexican
Quarters.

Men's Work

When the Bents and St. Vrain decided to build their fort on the northern bank of the Arkansas River, they traveled across the river to Mexico, specifically Taos, and recruited laborers to do the work for building the fort. They hired Mexican masons with the skills to take clay, prairie grasses dried to straw, sand, and water to make the adobe bricks. The contents were placed in a large pit, and oxen were used to grind the mixture. Mexican laborers packed the adobe mixture into adobe molds. Hundreds and hundreds of adobe bricks were made to build Bent's Fort.

To make the bricks, water had to be hauled. Sand and dirt used had to be sifted to rid it of large particles and also hauled to the building site. After the bricks were formed, they had to be stacked and dried before the laborious task of building began. Mexican laborers were kept busy full-time repairing and patching walls, interior and exterior, with this same adobe mud. This work was done using their hands. It was a constant labor.

Mexicans were also hired to take care of the livestock and other menial jobs. All those laborers had to be fed; that was women's work.

Women's Work - Food Preparation

The majority of the cooking for the laborers was done outside in front of their quarters. The fuel used for cooking and warmth was cottonwood found in abundance along the Arkansas River and buffalo dung found wherever buffalo had roamed. The buffalo dung, commonly know as chips, had to be completely dehydrated and dried by the sun before burning. As buffalo have a diet of grasses, chips burned easily and gave off heat. A very shallow pit was scored out on the ground and surrounded with a single layer of adobe bricks. The center of the pit was filled with large chopped cottonwood blocks and allowed to burn down to coals, providing the heat for cooking.

Two meals were prepared and served a day: breakfast at 10:00 a.m. and supper at 3:00 p.m. The meals were simple and nutritious. According to the article by Enid Thompson, one visitor to Bent's Fort wrote that meals were served in shifts of eight to twenty people.

The family, visiting dignitaries, and high ranking military guests ate first. The tables would be cleared; then lower ranking people, such as traders and trappers, ate in the dining room, minus some items such as bread. Resident craftsmen and ordinary employees ate in the plaza. Mexican laborers fixed their own food and ate outside their quarters. Mexican meals were eaten while sitting on the floor.

Cooking over the pit fire in the plaza.

Kitchen fire. The rectangular sheet, called the comal, used in making tortillas, is leaning on the right side of the fireplace.

Bent's Fort had its own cook, Charlotte Green who prepared the meals for trappers, hunters, and special guests. The Mexican laborers were great in number at the fort, but they had no rank over Charlotte. Charlotte and her husband Dick Green were black slaves owned by Charles and William Bent. Charlotte claimed to be "the only real lady in the whole Indian country."

Her domain was the kitchen and dining room, where she prepared and served meals and entertained. The dining room was the largest room of the fort. It was not only used for meals, but was a place of social gatherings such as fandangos, or dances.

Not much was written about Charlotte other than her being famous for her "slapjacks" and pumpkin pies. Charlotte had a pie safe in the room she shared with her husband, which was located between the kitchen and dining room. The pie safe was also used to store the Bents' water crackers produced by a Bent cousin in Massachusetts. The Greens had been Bent family slaves in Missouri. The Greens were given their freedom prior to William Bent's abandoning the fort.

The dining room did not have a fireplace. Instead, it had a brazier in the center of the room, which was filled with hot rocks in the winter for warmth. The dining room also had a large wooden dining table. A large white tablecloth was spread on it when meals were served. Charlotte had the largest fireplace and a large hearth in the kitchen, where she prepared meals.

Atole was the mainstay for breakfast. It was a gruel, a thin porridge made with ground cornmeal, hot water, milk, and raw brown sugar (*piloncillo*). It was prepared in the kitchen in a large pit in the plaza close to the kitchen or in front of the Mexican Laborers' Quarters. Suppers would vary, but one staple was tortillas, used for eating frijoles and other foods. A mano and *metaté* were used for grinding corn. To prepare the corn for grinding, it was cooked in simmering water with lime added to release the hulls and partially soften the corn. This is called *nixtamal*. The final product looks like hominy. The moist meal is called *masa*. The *masa* is patted into a thin tortilla and baked on a *comal*. This is a rectangular flat metal sheet with a flat handle at the end. The *comal* is heated on a bed of hot coals.

In the spring, a special delicacy was prepared with *nopales*. A *nopale* is a prickly pear cactus found in abundance outside the fort. The delicacy is the new growth of the cactus. The pads are gathered by cutting them off the mother plant with a sharp knife. Once there is a bucket full of cactus pads, they are soaked in water for a couple of hours to soften the prickles. Using a large, slightly sloped rock for a base, one by one the prickles are removed and the pods are sliced into *nopalitos*. The sliced pads are put in an iron kettle with boiling water. As the cactus cooks, a foamy, slimy film forms on top. It takes 20 minutes to cook. Then, the pads are thoroughly rinsed several times, after which all liquid is drained off and put in a wooden bowl ready for seasoning with salt, chopped onion, chopped garlic, and chili flakes. The *nopalitos* are used in scrambled eggs. Very tasty and good for you!

Alejandra removing seeds from chili pods
to be used as chili flakes for *nopalitos*.

Mexican Relationships with Others at the Fort

In the fall of 1845, a young invalid arrived at the fort to recuperate from an illness. His name was Francis Preston Blair, Jr., but the Bents called him Frank. He was a highly educated scholar. He made a fast recovery from his illness.

During the long December nights, Frank played his banjo. Charlotte, the fort's cook, and others gathered in the dining room for music, dancing, and taffy pulls. Charlotte made the candy using New Orleans molasses. Mexican laborer women watched the activities but could not participate.

The fort had a racetrack on the west side of the fort. Mexican laborer women were not allowed to witness any of the races of horses, mules, or donkeys.

The Mexican laboring woman I was portraying most likely had minimal interaction with Charlotte in the kitchen. Charlotte had social status and was well treated by the Bents. Her room had a double bed and a washstand with washbowl and ewer. Her quarters had a fireplace with a swing-out crane to hang cooking implements. Charlotte's assistant was most likely her husband Dick.

Bent's Fort housed several full-time staff including carpenters, a blacksmith, gunsmith, wheelwright, cook, and tailor. The lesser staff were considered non-permanent and included herders, adobe workers, horse wranglers, and hunters.

While I was working at the reconstructed fort, Richard Medina was a permanent fort employee portraying a Mexican laborer. He tended to all the livestock, including horses, oxen, peafowl, chickens, goats, cats, and buffalo. Richard also split the cottonwood used in all the fireplaces, hornos, and outdoor fire pits. During his portrayal he assisted me, the Mexican woman laborer, in cooking, adobe making, and in cleaning living quarters.

Richard Medina, fort laborer, standing between two oxen.

Trappers

Visiting the fort were resident trappers. One of the upper rooms on the west side of the fort was the Trappers' Quarters. Bent, St. Vrain and Company employed trappers. As employees, these men were bound to turn their furs over to the company, while the "free trappers" sold their furs to the company. The types of furs sold included beaver, otter, muskrat, badger, and bobcat. These trappers stayed long enough at the fort to get re-outfitted and do a little carousing.

Along the west side of the fort's lower level were three storage warehouses with the largest one in the middle, which had a raised entry to a lower storage area.

The first warehouse—the one with a circular pit—was used for furs ready for transport back East. The furs were buffalo robes bundled using the fur press in the center of the plaza. A "bundle" was ten buffalo robes, beaver pelts, muskrat and other hides.

In exchange for their furs, the trappers traded for new beaver traps, ammunition, coffee, tobacco, lead, bullet molds, blankets, and other supplies essential to their way of life.

Before heading back to the mountains, the trappers found time to lie back and "raise a little hell" during the visit. Imagine a free trapper coming in the main entrance to the fort, his mule packed with mostly beaver pelts to sell to the fort. Looking down at the mules' hooves, he would see the animal was in great need of having the shoes removed and the hooves trimmed. That was a good job for the blacksmith. A good time to do this job was while the mule was tired and more apt to stand still.

The women of the fort would have little or no interaction with the trappers. But why would they want to? After so long on the trail they were dirty, with hair in a mass of long tangled strands; beards needing trimming and shaping. It is obvious they chewed tobacco. Tobacco juice drooled on the sides of their mouths. Clothing would be tattered. What a sight to behold! To top it off, their language was hard for a Mexican woman to understand. And finally, the Mexican women were from good Catholic families and stayed together.

Once the free trapper turned his mule and extra horse over to the blacksmith, his next stop was the well room to get good ice-cold water. His needs would consist of a new red flannel shirt, new beaver traps to replace the ones the beaver got away with or broke, and other items already mentioned. After some time of enjoying civilized life at the fort and getting outfitted with the goods needed, he returned to the mountains for another season of trapping.

In 1845-46, the beaver trade declined due to over-trapping and because the beaver hat, so fashionable in Europe and eastern America, had been replaced by the silk hat.

Every spring, for several seasons, Bent's Old Fort hired a seasonal trapper-interpreter. Dan Muldoon was one hired. It was a pleasure getting to know him. Dan fully researched his character, achieving perfection in correct clothing, accouterments, and behavior, as far as I was concerned. He was the epitome of the trappers and traders.

On the upper level of the south side of the fort was the billiard room with a bar and a very large billiard table. One of the pleasures the trappers enjoyed was gambling, along with chewing tobacco and drinking Taos Lightning, a local brand of whiskey.

The trappers entertained one another by sharing their stories of where they had been and what they had seen. The storytelling was often exaggerated to make their experiences more dramatic.

Fort Interpreter Dan Muldoon as the resident
trapper lights his pipe at Alejandra's fire.

Although the Mexican laborer woman's contacts with the trappers was incidental, her main concern was to stay a distance from these rough-looking, grubby, outspoken, and mostly drunk men. Mexican women were dedicated to their men.

The Craftsman at the Fort

The craftsman's main job was to keep the wagons, oxen, and mules in top condition to continue travel on the Santa Fe Trail. Not only were those vehicles and livestock belonging to the fort needing maintenance, but also those stopping as they made their way along the trail.

The shoes of the oxen and mules had to be removed, their hooves trimmed, rasped and smoothed before new shoes could be replaced. The wheels of the wagons with broken spokes or felloes had to be replaced. These were jobs for the craftsman.

Staff and volunteers make life come alive at Bent's Fort.

Important Visitors to the Fort

War was in the air involving the Mexican laborer's country—
Mexico! In 1846, the United States sent troops to Bent's
Fort as an advance base for the Army of the West. In July, Colonel
Stephen Watts Kearny arrived at the fort with approximately 300
dragoons and over 1,000 Missouri Volunteers. Others visited the
fort in the same year.

Susan Magoffin at the Fort

Two other guests at the fort were Samuel and Susan Magoffin
traveling in a special carriage on their way to Santa Fe. Samuel
was a successful trader. Upon arrival at the fort, the northwest
corner room of the upper level was assigned to them. The room
has two windows, one looking out on the north prairie and the
other looking down toward the plaza. They traveled with their own
personal furniture, and that was the furniture used to furnish the
room assigned to them.

Susan Magoffin is important to the fort because of her written
descriptions of conditions and life during her stay. She was a newly
wedded wife, 18 years old and pregnant, yet she took the time to

keep a meticulous diary on her travels from Independence, Missouri, to Santa Fe, New Mexico, later published as *Down the Santa Fe Trail and Into Mexico.*

While her room was being furnished, based on her diary, the council room downstairs, where she waited, was described as a parlor with sparse furnishings. On July 30, 1846, Susan celebrated her 19th birthday and later had a miscarriage. Her child was buried somewhere outside the fort, location now unknown.

She wrote about a Mexican woman combing through her hair with some kind of oil or grease from a crock. Susan found it to be disgraceful. Susan also gave an account of an Indian woman giving birth to a baby boy in the room below her room, in the Mexican Quarters. She witnessed mother and child going to the river to bathe within a half hour or so after the birth. These are two stories that reflect the differences between cultures and the lack of understanding at the time.

Although her stay was brief, she took note of the noise in the plaza and surrounding area: horses being shod, braying of mules, crying of children, and men settling their differences.

The Mexican laborer woman's relationship with Susan Magoffin was minimal, if any contact was ever made. Both parties—travelers and laborers—probably did a lot of staring and wondering about each other.

Only twice during my tenure was Susan Magoffin portrayed by an interpreter for 12 days, the length of time and dates she spent at the fort. Susan was traveling with her husband Samuel en route to Santa Fe. She was the first Anglo woman documented as having been at Bent's Fort. She did give a good description of the Council Room with the rooms having dirt floors and how they had to be sprinkled with water to harden them and keep the dust down.

Due to her pregnancy, she was probably irritable about the noise in the plaza, not only the blacksmith's hammering, the neighing, and braying of livestock, but also the crying of children, and likely the outspoken carrying-on of trappers telling their tales of adventures in the mountains.

During Winter Quarters (an education event held at the reconstructed fort), it was difficult to portray Susan's stay at the fort accurately because she came in mid-summer. Winter Quarters has always been (as the name implies) in the winter.

Fort employees and volunteers outside the Mexican Quarters, including seasonal employee portraying Susan Magoffin, left.

Lieutenant James W. Abert

Lt. James Abert, U. S. Topographical Engineer, stayed at the fort twice, once in 1845, traveling with explorer John C. Fremont on an exploring expedition, and again in 1846, traveling with Colonel Stephen Watts Kearny, mapping the West as he traveled.

His journals included both written and graphic descriptions of the fort site, which left the most detailed and accurate accounts.

Particularly, during his stay in 1846, he sketched and measured the structure, providing an outline of the fort with dimensions.

Lt. Abert was also an artist who did two watercolor paintings of the interior of the fort. One is of the council room with Indians sitting on buffalo robes and a trader sitting on a wooden bench. The scene is a council between the Cheyenne and Delaware Indians. The other watercolor was of the Cheyenne scalp dance victory over the Pawnee Indians. He describes the dancers as numbering approximately 40 women with their faces painted red and black and wearing Navajo blankets.

Lt. Abert stayed in St. Vrain's quarters, which stood by itself above the cook's quarters and kitchen on the southeast side of the plaza. It was handy to the dining room, with winding stairs to the floor below.

Bent's Old Fort - The Decline

When the U. S. government sent troops to Mexico, via the Mountain Branch of the Santa Fe Trail, they headed to Bent's Fort. William Bent was asked by the government to designate the fort as an advance base for Stephen Watts Kearny's invasion into New Mexico.

The Mexican-American War was a conflict between the United States and Mexico, fought from April 1846 to February 1848. The main cause of the conflict stemmed from the annexation of the Republic of Texas by the U.S. and a dispute over the borders between Texas and Mexico. The war was hard on Bent's Fort.

Every inch of the fort was needed to house the dignitaries traveling with the government caravan headed toward Mexico. The government needed storage for the army supplies and rooms for the sick soldiers suffering from dysentery and scurvy. Some would die from their illnesses.

A quartermaster was left at the fort as the army traveled forward. His job was to keep inventory and care for the military supplies.

Upon the arrival of the Army of the West, the atmosphere became a nightmare. Due to the influx of the increased population of the military, the fort was severely impacted. The grass was overgrazed and the water holes were polluted. Tents were stretched for miles along the Arkansas River.

William Bent was having to supply storage and manpower to repair the wagons and care for the animals to get the Army back on the trail. William assigned the Army the largest of the three warehouses in the fort. The government never compensated him for the use of the fort, employees, and materials. The fort was used as a hospital and served as a government supply depot. All employees of the fort were used to accommodate the Army.

With the Army at the fort, most trade with the Native Americans ceased, causing financial problems for the Bents.

Charles Bent was in close touch with Americans who were interested in possible expansion in the west. After the United States took Santa Fe, Kearney, now promoted in rank to General, appointed Bent as the 1st American governor of New Mexico. Unfortunately, four months later, in 1847, Charles Bent was killed and mutilated during the Taos revolt. In 1849, William Bent and Ceran St. Vrain dissolved their partnership. Ceran returned to New Mexico and William remained at the fort, each carrying on in the businesses he knew best. They did try, unsuccessfully, to sell the fort to the U.S. government, but a price could not be settled.

In 1849, a cholera epidemic killed about half of the Southern Cheyenne population. William Bent moved to a better location near Big Timbers where the U.S. Government was using a by-pass over the Cimarron cutoff for mail delivery causing less traffic to the old Bent's Fort.

Some sources believe that William Bent blew up the fort by exploding kegs of gunpowder, placing the kegs in strategic areas of the fort and setting them on fire. Records show that the fort remained a post run by others for quite some time. There are accounts of other wagon trains that used the fort for refuge as they passed the area. Edward F. Beale, an ex-Navy officer, heading for California to assume his duties as an Indian agent, had his young cousin Gwinn Heap keep a journal of the 1853 trip:

May 31 – Swarms of mosquitoes prevented much sleep. En-
camped three miles above Bent's Fort. We rode all through
the ruins, which presented a strange appearance in these soli-
tudes. A few years ago this post was frequented by numerous
trappers and Indians, and at times exhibited a scene of wild
confusion . . . The adobe walls are still standing and are in
many places of great thickness. They are covered with written messages from parties who had already passed here to
their friends in the rear; they all stated that their herds were in
good condition, and progressing. — *Gwinn W. Heap, Central
Route to the Pacific* (Philadelphia, Penn: Lippincott, Grambo,
1854), pp.24-25.

A.E. Reynolds, who would later own the land where the old
fort stood, stated that William Bent didn't destroy the fort. He left
Indian dependents who did not want to move to the new fort in
charge. Records show that the strong adobe walls stood for many
years. Reynolds believed local ranchers began carrying off the
adobe bricks of the fort for other uses.

The fort was built for trading but had two towers for defense.

Living History Activities at the Fort

There is always something happening at Bent's Fort; it is active today as it was at the height of its trading days. Each year there are activities planned to give people a "hands-on" experience: Frontier Skills Day, Santa Fe Trail Encampment, Kids' Quarters, Fur Trade Encampment, and fun at the holidays. There is always the hiking trail and just historically visiting the fort and using your imagination to transport you in time. I was lucky to be involved with many of these activities.

Kids' Quarters

There is very little documentation of children's presence and their activities within the fort compound. Children found at the fort were most likely Mexican, families of the laborers.

Once a year, a special event, "Kids' Quarters," is held for children between the ages of seven and eleven years old. During the event, children spend half a day learning and being involved with such "hands-on" activities as doing chores, cooking, trading, and playing games. This was a "team effort" on the part of fort staff to bring young visitors into appreciation of the rebuilt fort and experience the labor-intensive hands-on activity.

All the children were intrigued with my portrayal of life at the fort, especially the adobe brick making and the labor involved.

One thing learned when working with children is they really like to be creative. They enjoyed learning to make tortillas and find out how creative it can be to cook without modern conveniences. When it came to rolling out the dough, they had to use broom handles as their rolling pins. Needless to say, the round tortillas that they are accustomed to ended up coming out in various shapes, like the State of Texas or California. It didn't matter; eating what they made was the best part. Homemade always taste better.

Making Adobe Bricks

In the spring, school groups are scheduled to tour the fort. The children are mostly 4th graders. The majority of the school groups come from Colorado, and Kansas. The school groups visiting from Kansas visit La Junta via AMTRAK and are transported by bus to the fort.

A demonstration of adobe making is the activity most requested by scout troops and grade schools. At Bent's Old Fort, the location chosen to re-enact the activity is the east side corral. A small circular pit is dug ankle deep, large enough for two people to stand and move inside. I enjoyed working with the children.

The first thing I would teach and show the children was putting the wooden mold in a large barrel filled with water to soak. Wood has to be completely saturated with moisture to facilitate the adobe bricks to slip out cleanly when they are completed. The mold is in the form of a box with four-inch-deep sides.

As part of the experience, I would lead the small group of students to gather the needed materials. All materials are collected as they walk to the nearby Arkansas River carrying several buckets. As they walk, the children would sometimes spot a mule deer camouflaged within the cottonwood trees or hear a bobwhite quail. Once they saw a killdeer; it seemed to be guarding something—perhaps its chicks—as we were intruding in its territory. Noisy black and white magpies would fly toward the cottonwood trees along with lots of gnats and mosquitoes, of course. Every now and then, a grasshopper buzzed by.

At the river I would show them freshly chopped cottonwood trees. Yes, those are a beaver's teeth marks on the stump.

Then we got to work. We would locate an area by the river where the sand was dry, easily accessible, and free of debris. They filled the wooden bucket they carried halfway with sand. Then, heading back, a loose pile of rich soil accommodated the need for that ingredient. We fill three buckets with that. The last bucket would be filled halfway with prairie grass.

Back at the fort, the soil was put in the pit. On top of the soil, the sand was added, and then the prairie grass, or straw, if that is available. Finally, water from the cistern would be added in the pit.

Mixing adobe with a volunteer student during the Kid's Quarters event. Photo courtesy of the *La Junta Tribune-Democrat*.

The adobe mold that has been soaking is set on the dampened ground near the pit. With their hands, the adobe mold is filled to the top with the adobe mixture. The mixture is smoothed even to the top of the mold with wet hands. Once the mud in the mold is completely compacted, with all air bubbles erased and smoothed, the mold is immediately lifted. What is left on the moist ground is a rectangular adobe brick. The adobe brick will be sun dried or cured, and will be turned periodically so all sides dry. It was good for the children to see how hard it was to make one brick, then imagine making hundreds of these adobe bricks.

I will always remember the children's reaction to the adobe-making activity. Their eyes glowed with anticipation. Their giggling was nervous when asked who would volunteer to get in the pit. Once in the pit, with some of the comments you could feel their joy as they said it feels weird or the water is cold. The big worry was if the mud would come off their feet. But most of all, "This was fun!" What a perfect way to teach children through experiences. There were never any mud fights, which might be expected. I think the children did learn, when brought into perspective, how much work and contribution the laborers brought to Bent's Fort.

In mass production for the construction of a large structure such as Bent's Fort, mules or oxen were used to do the mixing. Once the adobe bricks were dried, they were stacked in a systematic order so air could be circulated throughout the stack to continue the drying process until they would be used.

Bent, St. Vrain and Company designed the plans for the adobe fort, relying on Mexican laborers and masons to make and build the adobe bricks.

The purpose of this activity was to replicate an adobe brick using a mold of the size and type employed in construction of Bent's Fort in the early 1800s. The brick measures 18 inches in length, nine inches wide, and four inches thick—the same dimensions as the bricks used in construction of the original fort and now in the reconstruction.

Winter Quarters

Winter Quarters, offered at Bent's Old Fort, is a special event that demonstrates life in a fur trading post. It is an event that gives the visiting public an opportunity to see a "living history" program in action. All visitors are welcomed to participate in this "hands-on" activity.

Winter Quarters is an annual program designed to provide graduate-level learning for history professionals, interpreters, and teachers through practical living experiences. It is also designed to give teachers the opportunity to receive recertification.

The fort staff, seasonal fort interpreters, regular fort volunteers, journalists, artists, school teachers, college professors, and historical re-enactors come together to recreate life at a fur trading post as it was nearly two centuries ago.

Prior to the participants' arrival, they are given a list of books which it is suggested they read to prepare for interaction with visitors and enable them to answer basic questions on the history of Bent's Old Fort.

A half-day classroom training is designed to outline the goals and objectives of the event. Immediately after the training, the participants are assigned to character roles. Each group is led by a Park Service permanent or seasonal staff member.

I led the domestic laborers group gathering in the Mexican living quarters. Permanent park staff employees, such as the blacksmith and carpenter, are assigned living quarters between the blacksmith and carpenter shops, in the south end of the plaza. Trappers stay in the Trappers' Quarters, and dragoons stay in the Military Quarters, both located on the upper level overlooking the plaza.

Participants are required to dress in period clothing, eat from period utensils, and speak of period events. Winter Quarters usually takes place in the month of March.

One thing I was happy to participate in was a plan I implemented as part of the Winter Quarters event. I suggested giving the participants a real historical camping experience north of the fort! Of course, I had scouted an area on private property about two miles or less from the fort and knew the land owner who gave us permission to use it as a training experience for adults. My idea was accepted by the park superintendent. All Set!

Summary of the First Winter Quarters Camp

Prior to leaving for the campsite, instructions were given for rolling up buffalo robes before loading them on the freight wagon.

Buffalo robes rolled, laid out and ready for beds at Winter Quarters.

Upon arrival at the campsite, the north winds started to interfere with setting up camp, which we finally managed to do. However, the cooking was postponed. The first exercise was gathering the materials for a fire and starting it with flint and steel. Of course, we only went through the motions of fire starting due to the high winds. We had to settle for hard tack, Bent's water crackers, jerky, and water.

There were approximately 20 participants total, including the instructors on the camp-out. We all slept on buffalo robes. The ladies had four to share among them, and the men had the same number. The trappers were assigned to stand guard throughout the night. Only the modern essentials were taken with us, such as medicines for people who needed them and lots of water and snacks and juice for diabetics.

The privy was an area a short distance from camp. For "number two," a small hole was dug and covered after use.

The men wore brogans on their feet. Most of the women had leather mocs so they could feel the rocky terrain underfoot.

The ladies camped near the freight wagon for protection from the wind, although the wind did calm down sometime during the night. Fort interpreter Greg Holt camped near the oxen in order to keep them close to camp.

I don't think anyone got much sleep at camp due to the excitement of the experience, the wind howling, and tumbleweeds moving around.

Finally, as soon as day broke, all were ready to return to Bent's Fort. Even the oxen had a faster pace. It was a beautiful sight to see that magnificent fort at a distance with the cottonwood trees in the background. It was worth the trip to give a small flavor of the trail and seeing the fort at a distance. Back at the fort, breakfast was served at 10 a.m. There were many jobs to do during the day during Winter Quarters.

Fire Starting Using Flint and Steel

It is essential for traders and trappers that a tinder box containing a steel, a flint, and char cloth was in their possession at all times. During my interpretive role at the fort, I kept mine in a leather pouch. Needed to start a fire would be dried prairie grass, wood shavings from the carpenter shop, and leftover kindling from splitting wood.

Prior to starting the fire, thin slats of cottonwood or pine are laid tepee-style toward the back of the fireplace so the flame will be drawn up the chimney once the fire is ignited.

All is set. We are ready to start the fire with flint, steel, and char cloth. Make a bird nest with the prairie grass and wood shavings. Position the cloth under the flint. Strike the fire steel on the flint's outer edge to send sparks flying. Once the sparks ignite the char cloth, they are caught in the prepared nest. A few puffs of breath will set the nest aflame. Lastly, the nest is placed in the fireplace to ignite the larger pieces of wood.

Fire starting kit containing steel , flint, and char cloth.

The Winter Quarters crowd tried their hands at starting fires in the kitchen, craftsman's quarters, Mexican quarters, military quarters with the taught method. All these rooms required fires daily for cooking. I thoroughly enjoyed working side by side with these new learners, although one of my hardest tasks was to assure they were safe, especially from the coals catching their clothes on fire.

All cooking was done with coals. The only time a fire flame was useful was when the tin reflector oven was used for roasting.

Once all instructors and Winter Quarters participants were in the assigned quarters, the groceries were handed out. Because the fort had chickens, everyone got eggs. The ledgers show slabs of bacon. Everyone got bacon. Each of the quarters' participants got a tin coffee pot, and everyone had his or her tin coffee cup. In a bag marked "coffee" were coffee beans which had to be ground.

The Mexican laborer group added tortillas to their breakfast. The dragoons added hard tack, which was a hard biscuit. The trappers and traders ate in the dining room, where the meals cooked by the domestics were served.

Milking the Cow and Making Butter

During the Winter Quarters, as a representative of the Mexican laborers, I had to milk the cow first thing prior to breakfast. Then came another chore, making butter.

Milking the cows on a cold morning. Notice the laborers are in their blanket coats. Photograph by Barbara Van Cleve©1983

Milking a cow presented a real challenge to the ladies. I had brought a milk cow from my ranch for Winter Quarters to participate in the activities. Although I knew the cow was safe, for the ladies there was a real fear factor. They were truly afraid of being kicked. Learning how to draw milk from the udders is challenging. Some thought they were hurting the cow.

Before putting the dasher in the stone churn to make butter, it is rubbed with salt. The salt is used to prevent the fat from sticking to the dasher. It is a long and tedious job working the dasher up and down, up and down until the butter comes. At first the cream becomes a thick whipped cream. Gradually, it separates into lumpy, small, yellow bits, and the buttermilk comes. Many of the Winter Quarters participants had a taste of fresh "homemade" buttermilk.

A pan with water is for washing the butter before packing the butter into the mold. It may be necessary to wash the butter as many as four times to remove all the buttermilk. The water should be clear before you stop working the butter. Then the butter is packed in the butter mold. The mold is wood and oblong. The butter is used immediately, and what is left, if any is left, is covered with a dampened cheesecloth. It was such a treat for the participants that it was inhaled when served on biscuits.

Churning butter during the Winter Quarters in a tall stone churn. Alejandra is pressing excess buttermilk from the butter.

Baking and Roasting Using the Horno

An horno is a beehive-shaped adobe oven. At Bent's Old Fort, it was located outside the east inner corral next to the kitchen's back door. In order to bake or cook in the horno, a fire had to be started early in the morning.

A long-handled wooden paddle was used to put baking or cooking goods in the horno. The horno has a fitted front door made of wood and lined with burlap inside. Overnight, the door is put in the cistern to soak before it is used. Early in the morning, a fire is started in the horno and fed wood for at least three to four hours. After the horno is cleaned, the food to be baked is placed inside, the horno door is placed in the front, and the horno is completely sealed, including the air vent.

Preparing the horno for the buffalo hind quarter.

Winter Quarters participants were not disappointed when they were served the buffalo roast cooked in the horno. Almost 100% of the participants had never tasted buffalo meat. It was a treat for them. They compared the taste and texture of the meat to beef.

Preparing the Skinned Buffalo for Eating

The trappers, traders, and hunters worked hard to process their prize, the buffalo. It requires slaughtering, butchering, and fleshing the hide, all hard and time consuming labor.

All four corners of the paunch are secured to the notched lodge poles by placing a slit cut in the hide in all four corners. Buffalo stew meat is cooked inside.

Using the Stomach Paunch of the Buffalo as a Cooking Vessel

Once the paunch, the large stomach, was removed from the rest of the intestines, it was immediately emptied of its contents and soaked in a water barrel with a handful of lime to help release the impurities. It took many rinses to become clean enough to use as a cooking vessel. Cooking in the paunch was possible after it was suspended from four waist-high corner posts driven into the ground. The four corners of the paunch were secured to the notched posts.

Once the paunch is thoroughly clean inside, water is poured into it, and one by one, hot rocks are put into the water. It takes three or four rocks to start the water boiling. Then, buffalo meat is cut into stew size pieces and dropped in the paunch with a couple more rocks. The meat will attach itself to the hot rocks. Immediately, one at a time, the rocks will be retrieved using an iron dipper that has holes to drain the water. The meat is then peeled off the rocks. The meat is cooked rare, and with a sprinkle of salt is ready to eat.

Alejandra starts fleshing the hide by pulling the flesh up in order to get underneath it with her Green River knife, the same that the hunters used during the early 19th century.

Fleshing the Buffalo Hide

The Indians used every part of the buffalo. At the fort, the resident trapper takes the wet buffalo hide, spreads it on the plaza ground, and uses wood pegs to hold the stretched hide in place for scraping off any soft flesh remaining on the carcass. At the fort it was not tanned, but the hide was allowed to dry and be used as rawhide.

Setting Up a Jerky Rack for Drying Buffalo Meat

In the fall of 1993, Bent's Old Fort purchased a buffalo hide tepee. The 14-foot tepee was constructed by Larry Beliz of Hot Springs, South Dakota. Bent's Old Fort purchased the hides, 18-foot lodge poles, lacing pins, pegs, and a hide-tying rope. A jerky rack was a tripod with small lodge poles placed horizontally, about four feet from the ground and secured to the upright poles with soft rawhide straps. The straps are tied as one would use sisal rope today to tie things together. Jerky is buffalo meat cut in long, thin strips and hung out to dry on a rack similar to the one described above.

Preparing the rack for drying jerky with tepee in background.

Women Portraying Indians at Winter Quarters

William Bent handled the Indian trade on-site at the fort, or they were reached by traders traveling to the Indian camps. The tribes were the Southern Cheyenne, Arapaho, Kiowa, and many others.

A Winter Quarters participant portrays a Native American grinding dried berries.

Entertainment at the Fort: Winter Quarters Finale

The final event for Winter Quarters was the fandango, a Spanish dance. Most Mexican people are naturally musical and love to dance. One of their instruments of choice is the violin.

The 19th century Santa Fe trader Lewis Garrard tells about Rosalie, a half breed French and Indian squaw whose husband Ed was the fort carpenter. She and Charlotte, the famed fort cook, were led to the floor of the dining room "to trip the light fantastic toe," whirling about in an American backwoods dance.

Also, a young Francis Preston Blair, Jr., convalescing at the fort, played his banjo and told of Mexican and French Canadians gathered in the big dining room and described how half-breed Rosalie and black Charlotte "queened" it over Mexican and Indian women who could only stare at the whirling convolutions of the backwoods American dancers.

During Winter Quarters the dining room floor was cleared for the fandango. No one in the group played violin or banjo. Music was provided by the Mariachi group who played monthly at Our Lady of Guadalupe/St. Patrick parish in La Junta, Colorado, although the music was not of the Bent's Fort period.

It was my idea for the women to get a flour and water facial. Susan Magoffin recorded that the New Mexico women wore rice powder paste on their faces, which made them look like corpses.

There were plenty of "hailstorms" to go around amongst the Winter Quarters participants. A "hailstorm" is whiskey, sugar, mint, and ice in a glass jar. All ingredients were available at the fort. The whiskey was used sparingly. The wild mint came from the nearby Purgatory River.

Women after the flour and water facial getting ready for the fandango.

The end of the fandango marked the conclusion of Winter Quarters. Some of the trappers and traders took off to the billiard room of the fort, while others stayed and visited under the veranda that circled the plaza. A real "hands-on" experience was coming to an end.

One thing I remember working Winter Quarters was when evening came, all domestics were ready for bed. They were so tired from doing tedious work and standing long hours. So, lying on the buffalo robe felt good. The remark or comment I heard most was, "This is hard work physically." There are some participants that will never forget the lives of the Mexican women who labored at Bent's Fort.

Winter Quarters participants worked a full day. One job was plucking a chicken, washing and dressing it, and then cooking the chicken. Photograph by Barbara Van Cleve©1983.

On a winter day at the fort, Winter Quarters participants stand with fort employees. The oxen and conestoga wagon are fort regulars.

Animals at the Fort

The Santa Fe Trail began at Independence, Missouri, which was the chief outfitting point for trading caravans. Bent's Fort was on the Mountain Branch of the Trail. The mountain route was longer, passing over Raton Pass into New Mexico, but it was also safer and had an easier road.

Oxen

Freight wagons were pulled by oxen and later by mules. Charles Bent introduced oxen to the Trail for a few years before he started using mules.

After the fort's reconstruction in 1976, two pure bred Red Devon oxen were purchased for interpretation and demonstration by the fort's historical association. Then a second pair of purebreds, a pair of five-year-old Red Devon oxen, named Tom and Jerry, made their home at Bent's Old Fort. The oxen were delivered to the fort from Connecticut by Steve and Mike Bowers of Fort Collins, Colorado.

Oxen are castrated bulls which are trained in tandem to respond to both voice commands and the light flick of a whip.

Barb horses grazing in front of the fort.

Barb Horses at Bent's Fort

Barb horses are descendants of the Spanish barbs brought by the conquistadors to the New World. The original Spanish barb was a cross between horses brought by the Moors from the Barbary Coast of Africa and the Andalusian islands.

The Buffalo Heifer Huerfana

A baby buffalo was donated to the fort when its mama died from a cause unknown. Small as it was, it was still needing to nurse in order to live. My friend Roxie Hoss learned about the fort's dilemma and offered a solution to the problem. Roxie had a Nubian nanny goat for sale. The nanny had raised many calves.

The fort purchased the nanny goat and introduced "Nanny' to the buffalo calf, which the fort personnel named "Huerfana," which means orphan in Spanish. Huerfana immediately went to

Nanny, but Nanny had never seen a buffalo and started to run away. Huerfana pursued. She could smell Nanny's udder and wanted it. At first, Nanny had to be held so Huerfana could nurse.

Once the nanny and Huerfana bonded, plans were made to build a stanchion, an upright stand for Nanny to stand on while Huerfana nursed. This kept the buffalo calf from butting Nanny's udder quite so hard.

Once Huerfana was weaned, Nanny was held in the east inner corral of the fort, while Huerfana was kept in the large back corral. Nannies are natural mamas. Richard Medina, the fort laborer, was an excellent hand with the animals, big and small.

With good food and care, Huerfana grew large.

Special Events at the Fort

The Park Service is always willing to work with various groups to set up an event that will benefit each individual group's needs. Advance notice is needed to coordinate events, but the Park Service is always willing to work with groups.

Cheraw School Students Learn at the Fort

In 1992, the new eighth grade interdisciplinary learning program was introduced at the Cheraw School. The unit was built around a re-enactment of life in the 1840s at Bent's Old Fort. I worked closely with Principal Sheila Henry to prepare for the encampment. It involved traveling to the school to explain activities in which the students would participate. It was decided the students would make their own period clothing, created from patterns furnished by the fort.

The school group traveled to the fort by horse and wagon. A buffalo was donated to the school's project by Zapata Ranch in the San Luis Valley. The buffalo was butchered at my ranch by my husband Dell, and the students participated fully in the event.

Since it was an overnight occasion, the students experienced sleeping in a buffalo robe and cooking over the open fire.

My goal was to bring the students into the fort and give them "hands-on" knowledge of living history—to bring the story of the fort ALIVE !

Teachers Learn of Fort through University of Colorado Consortium

On another occasion, and prior to my retirement, teachers from eight states, a graduate-level group offered by the Social Sciences Education Consortium (a course offered at the University of Colorado at Boulder) experienced first-hand what it was like to live at the fort. The consortium was funded through the National Endowment for the Humanities. Project secretary Sylvia Thomas of Golden, Colorado, performed domestic chores during her stay. Of that experience, she commented, "People in the 1800s had a very hard life. I cooked breakfast and dinner, did the laundry, made candles, milked goats, and worked adobe. Women did not receive the appreciation they deserved."

Project director Jim Giese remarked, "[Bent's Old Fort] is such a great example of the confluence of cultures—a nice springboard."

Language arts teacher Leandra Marshall of San Mateo, California, said, "It was absolutely wonderful. Cooking over the open fire was really an experience."

I feel that the goals were fulfilled in bringing the fort alive with a "hands-on" living history program at this event. I'm proud to say that hard work produces results.

Santa Fe Trail Association Symposium, 1993

The Santa Fe Trail Association Symposium titled "A Corridor Through Time" was coordinated by three principal fort staff.

The Indian Encampment

Park Ranger Craig Moore handled the Indian Encampment. It

was one of the most popular events to take place at the fort. It was held southeast of the fort along the Arkansas River in the cottonwood grove, where several tepees and lean-tos were erected by frontier buffs. All participants wore period dress.

One of the speakers at the Indian encampment was George Sutton of Canton, Oklahoma. He was vice-chairman of the Medicine Wheel Coalition of North America and a member of the business committee for the Cheyenne and Arapaho tribes.

75th Anniversary of the National Park Service

This special event brought together the three men involved in the reconstruction of the fort and three direct descendants of Ceran St. Vrain, an owner of the original fort. Held August 24, 1991, the occasion commemorated the 75th anniversary of the National Park Service that was responsible for rebuilding the historic structure.

As part of this Diamond Jubilee of the fort, a large bronze plaque depicting Stephen P. Mather, founder of the NPS, was dedicated.

The three men involved in the fort's re-construction were Emil Gimeno, general contractor; Bob Smith, project supervisor; and George Thorson, historic architect. The descendants of St. Vrain attending were Mary Louis Gallegos of Belen, New Mexico, great granddaughter of St. Vrain, and her two daughters. This was the first time they had visited the fort their great-grandfather had constructed.

"I remember as a little girl my father saying Mother's great-grandfather was a famous man, but it wasn't until I became an adult that I really became interested in who he was or what he had done," said Felicia Marie (Gallegos) Moreland of Albuquerque.

Staff of Bent's Old Fort NHS, summer 1991, on south staircase leading to Billiard Room. Center in uniform is Fort Superintendent Don Hill. Below him is Chief Ranger Alejandra Aldred. The plaque honoring Stephen P. Mather, founder of the National Park Service, was dedicated as part of the Diamond Jubilee.

Lessons Learned Working at Bent's Fort

What I learned from portraying the Mexican laborer woman is that it doesn't matter what your social status is. The application of yourself to what is expected of you and doing the job with conviction, making it believable and having fun doing it, reveals

who you are. The photographs in the book speak for themselves and show an employee who took one aspect of her job, which was telling the story of the Mexican laborer woman and giving her a voice. I willingly tried to tell her important story and share it with the Bent's Fort staff and the visiting public. The secrets of my accomplishments are my "can-do attitude," belief in myself, acceptance of guidance from my supervisors, and capitalizing on every opportunity given to me. Last, but not least, I was ALWAYS a "team player."

Hungry trappers, traders, and hunters await a buffalo roast just out of the horno, which is being carved by Sam Arnold and Alejandra in the Fort dining room. Photograph by Barbara Van Cleve©1983.

Retirement Fall 1995

One of the highlights of my career was seeing the fort ruins rise from two dimensions to three dimensions: reconstruction. For the first seven years of my employment at the fort, I had the challenge of telling the story of the two-dimensional view of the fort. I found it hard to think three dimensions in telling the story.

The reconstruction helped me understand the scale and the appearance of the fort which enhanced my interpretation of this magnificent trading post for the visiting public for generations to come. The National Park Service mandates that interpreters are to educate visitors about life in the past. The reconstruction of the fort helps visitors understand the times. My goal was to tell this story in a compelling manner to each visitor. It is one thing to say Mexican men and women made adobe bricks, and another thing to show the vastness of the fort and marvel at the size and design of the building they originally helped design and build.

During the next 20 years of my employment, after the reconstruction, the fort experts sought historical accuracy, which was often hard to guarantee without documentation. During my tenure, many changes took place. Further research demanded correction. At the same time, other changes took place where existing structures presented possible safety hazards. Today, study, observation, and modifications are ongoing.

Regional Associate Director of the Denver Field Office Glen Bean (retired) wrote the following upon my retirement:

> "It has been with a great deal of pleasure, appreciation, and indeed affection, that I have followed your career at Bent's Old Fort. ...The role that you played in those early days as administrative clerk helped us to solve...problems. ...I do want to remind you lest you forget that the Regional office very much appreciated your sound judgment and wise counsel. ...I was so pleased when you moved into interpretation for you had demonstrated such a sensitive and realistic appreciation of the role of Bent's Old Fort in western history and how the story should be told to visitors and the local community."

From the Social Science Education Consortium (SSEC)'s Jim Giese, Barbara Miller, Sylvia Thomas, and Lori Eastman, "Thanks for helping us develop a deeper understanding of the American West. Your work with teachers is an important contribution of improving education."

From Maggie Johnston, Chief I & RM, Florissant Fossil Beds National Monument, "As one of Alejandra's colleagues...I think it is important to remember that people make the service and people like Alejandra have set the standard for the rest of us."

From Karen Whitney, Lake Mead National Recreation Area, "I still fondly remember you showing me around when [Bent's Old Fort] was just an outline on the ground. ...You have always been synonymous with Bent's [Fort] for me. I know that it is the great little place. It is largely through your efforts."

From Bill and Ida Featherstone, "How happy I've always been that I picked you to start your National Park Service career. ... Few people in the Park Service stayed at their assignment as long as you have, and few have seen changes as monumental as you—from a maze of excavated foot-high ruins to an imposing two-story structure!"

From Jere Krakow, Superintendent Long Distance Trail Office, Salt Lake City, Utah, "You have been a credit to the NPS, and I have appreciated your help through the years on the Santa Fe Trail work. Your manner with visitors and that most infectious smile will be missed by many."

Alejandra and Dell Aldred

My early retirement at the age of 53 was due to my husband Dell's being ill and requiring care. It wasn't long until my husband passed away. I was so blessed and thankful that I was at his side when he died.

Prior to his illness, we hosted the annual "Aldred Trail Ride." As a memorial to Dell, we had one last trail ride to scatter his ashes in a special place. It was a place where Dell had worked in his younger years on a ranch feeding cattle, located in Smith Canyon south of La Junta.

When Dell worked at the ranch, the cowboys would bring the "cottonseed cake" in a wagon pulled by a team of horses, and many times Dell had to wait for the arrival, so he kept himself busy by sketching his name and the date on a huge rock with a flat side.

One such writing was "DEL 6/33."

As part of our trip to scatter his ashes, we hauled our wagon and mule team and horses to Kelly and Randy Bader's ranch. They granted us permission to camp in their large corral. The next morning Harry Rosell hitched the wagon to the mules, and with me and Harry in the wagon, sitting on either side of Dell's ashes in a large Jack Daniels bottle, we were on our way to the site.

Lloyd and Edith Hall, well-known local musicians, sang a couple of hymns where we left Dell.

Mexican Laborer Woman Alejandra Speaks

W*elcome! My name is Alejandra. I am one of the Mexican laborer women. This room, where we are standing, is assigned to me and other laborers.*

Imagine eight to ten families in this room. Our bed is the buffalo robe, which is rolled up against the wall. We use it at night as our bed and during the day as chairs. You are welcome to sit on it, if you like.

Our meals are simple, but nutritious. Breakfast is prepared for serving at 10 a.m. and supper at 3:00 p.m. Before you are some of the implements for preparing meals. The mano and metate are used for grinding corn. The sheet metal is a comal used for baking our tortillas.

Hanging on the rail is my blanket, a Rio Grande pattern, and a pallet of straw for a mattress. I am Catholic. I have a simple wood cross, as you can see.

The wood you see in the fireplace is cottonwood. In hard times, when the cottonwood is scarce, I walk outside the fort walls and look for completely dried buffalo chips, which are flakes of buffalo dung. They burn just like wood and give heat and cook our meals, when necessary.

My room has two windows facing the plaza. The slats on the window frame are for keeping the chickens out, and the shutters are for privacy.

My dress is simple: a chemise and draw-string skirt. All my needs such as material for a new skirt or chemise, beans, sugar, etc., come from the trade room on credit. The head clerk keeps a record on a ledger. I do believe I will never pay off what I owe to the company store. Maybe one of you would like to pay my debt.

Soon, I will start a fire with flint and steel and a little char cloth. Let me show you how it's done, although we won't start the fire. I keep everything I need in this tinderbox. First, I will show you how you get the sparks. Hold the steel in your right hand and the flint in your left. Now, strike the steel on the flint. See the sparks? Now, I'm ready to put the char cloth on top of the flint. A spark will start the char cloth to burning. It's that easy.

The fire steels and flint are available in the trade room. These two items were traded to the Indians to replace the concept of rubbing sticks together to start a fire.

Please, check the first room after you leave me. It is a warehouse. It is the one after you leave the well room. Look in and you will see some furs hanging from the vigas. The floor is a large circular pit. My people would entertain themselves by having cock fights in there. Two roosters are put in the pit and wagers would be placed on which would win.

Thank you for your visit, and enjoy your stay.

How many times I gave this speech! Then the questions would follow. I only hope my answers gave the visitors a view of the importance of the Mexican women laborers at Bent's Fort, a voice for the women.

Life after Bent's Fort—My Adopted Son

Late in life, the Lord blessed me with an amazing son, the Reverend Alphonsus Ihuoma. Although my family members and friends showered me with special cards addressing and thanking me for being a mother to them at various times of the year, I felt grateful for their thoughtfulness, but my heart needed more.

When I first met Father Alphonsus, I immediately gravitated toward him in a motherly fashion when he served his appointment at Our Lady of Guadalupe/St. Patrick parish in La Junta, Colorado. Without hesitation or thought, I became accessible to him as he pursued his priestly ministry and academic studies. There are times in our struggles in life when God presents an opportunity for us to be of service to others with open hearts. The call came to me to be a MOM for this special priest from Onicha Ezinihitte Mbaise, Nigeria.

I witnessed my son's receiving his Master of Law in Natural Resources and Environmental Law and Policy at Strum College of Law at the University of Denver, Denver, Colorado, and his Doctor of Judicial Science. His dissertation title was "The Holy See, Social Justice and International Trade Law: Assessing the Social Mission of the Catholic Church in the GATT-WTO System" presented at the University of Kansas, Lawrence, Kansas.

I am a MOM, proud to have Rev. Dr. Alphonsus Ihuoma as my adopted son.

The following is a quote from my son's book titled "The Holy See, Social Justice, and International Trade Law":

"I am highly indebted to my mother, Alejandra Aldred-Adams, who stood behind me in all travails. When she came into my life and my priestly ministry, her life reaffirmed my belief that no matter how wicked the world may seem to be, there are still people out there who are honest, disciplined, gracious, God-fearing, loving and lovable. She has been a great inspiration in my priestly life and in all my academic pursuits since I came to the United States. I am proud to be her son. God will always bless and reward her abundantly."

About the Author, Alejandra's Story

Alejandra A. Aldred-Adams, tells her story from the perspective of a home-grown Hispanic female who worked at Bent's Old Fort National Historic Site for a little over a quarter of a century and witnessed monumental events there. She saw this historic location go from ruins to reconstruction in one year. She observed, first-hand, the old fort as it rose anew.

Keep in mind, she says, that "as a fort interpreter, I was a 20th century woman of Mexican heritage telling the story of a 19th century Mexican laborer, specifically a Mexican laborer woman. The people who built and maintained the fort were Mexican laborers who occupied the most menial jobs and lacked social standing at the fort. Yet, Mexican laborers were most likely the dominant group participating in everyday life at the fort. All menial jobs were carried out by this group, such as plastering walls, tending livestock, gathering wood, and hauling water. Very little has been written about these 'peons.' "

Education

Alejandra Adelaide Gonzales Aldred-Adams was born on March

20, 1943, in Swink, Otero County, Colorado. She was one of eighteen children, being number twelve.

In the year 1943, an acre of land was purchased by Alejandra's parents along U. S. Highway 50 west of La Junta, and a four room house was built using the same materials as the ones used for construction of Bent's Old Fort: adobe bricks. Today, the house is vacant, but it is still standing in the same location as 1943.

She attended West School grades one to six in nearby La Junta. When she began her schooling, she did not speak English, but thanks to Phil and Jean Ann Hudspeth and Tommy and Dorothy Richards, she learned. They tutored her during lunch hours.

She attended Herren Junior High School through grades seven and eight and was graduated from Swink Consolidated High School in 1962. She credits her perseverance to an award titled "I Dare You" created by William H. Danforth. Its philosophy was four-fold: "Think tall, stand tall, smile tall, live tall."

After high school, she attended Otero Junior College in La Junta with the intention of taking classes that would prepare her for a business career. Upon completion, she hoped to be employed locally as a bank teller, working her way up to an administrative position. However, with portfolio in hand, she interviewed with many businesses but had no luck.

Federal Civil Service Career

In 1964, she visited the La Junta Post Office and was encouraged by Postal Clerk Fern Waddlow to take the Federal Civil Service Test. She learned from Ms. Waddlow there was demand for Clerk Typists in Washington, D. C., and Ms. Waddlow would be offering the test in a few days. The test was given, and Alejandra passed.

Alejandra began her Federal Service career as a clerk (typing) temporary appointment, Pueblo Army Depot Property Division, Administrative Branch, Pueblo, Colorado, for six weeks in 1965. Soon, a call came from Washington, D.C.

Alejandra had been accepted for a career conditional appointment to start November 1, 1965. The position was that of a Clerk-Dictating-Machine Transcriber working for the Food and Drug Administration under the Bureau of Medicine, division of Medicine Information, Medical Literature Branch in Arlington, Virginia. Her duties were to transcribe in final form, from a Dictaphone belt, correspondence, memoranda, reports, etc., researched by librarians for a medical bulletin published quarterly on the side effects of oral contraceptives.

In July of 1966, she transferred to the Department of Justice, Bureau of Narcotics and Dangerous Drugs, at the Denver Field Office, Colorado. Here, she continued to work as a Clerk-Dictating Machine Transcriber. This position, too, involved transcribing and editing of highly technical reports for criminal investigations within the field office.

In 1968, she transferred to Fort Carson's headquarters of the 5th Infantry Division's Finance and Accounting Office as a Military Pay Clerk, a position which made her responsible for the pay of officers and enlisted military personnel.

Awards for Achievement Working at Bent's Fort

In the 1990s, Alejandra was promoted to Assistant Chief Ranger, and in 1995 she retired as Chief Ranger. During her 27 years of service at Bent's Old Fort she received the following awards:

UNIT AWARD– October 1972

The Unit Award was for bilingual assistance at the Second World Conference on National Parks. It was earned for my "marathon efforts" typing the Spanish versions of the conference recommendations. This required working in the wee hours of the morning and assisting in making the participants comfortable and welcome.

In the book titled *Preserving a Heritage: Final Report to the President and the congress of the National Parks Centennial commission, Washington, D.C.*, page 80, is a picture of Alejandra stationed at the registration area registering delegates to the Second World Conference of National Parks, a gathering of Nations at Yellowstone National Park.

OUTSTANDING PERFORMANCE RATING –April 1, 1974 to September 1977

The rating was for directing and coordinating all programs and activities of administrative function and serving as acting Park Superintendent seven years and coordinator of all programs and activities performed within the Interpretative Division from June to September 1977. This was during a period when the park visitation jumped from 39,479 in 1974 to 109,290 in 1975 and 90,202 in 1976, the park's highest visitor-use ever recorded because of the reconstruction of the fort.

QUALITY INCREASE AWARD – November 1977

The award was an outstanding performance for performing all the important functions of the position at a continuing high level of effectiveness.

SPECIAL ACHIEVEMENT AWARD – November 1983

The award was for working with two of four Barb horses donated to Bent's Fort. The horses were trained to be ridden. After 60 days of work, these two horses could be saddled and ridden as a part of the historic scene.

SPECIAL ACHIEVEMENT AWARD – October 1986

The award was for exceeding the normal requirements of the position by acting in the position of Chief Ranger June and July of 1986. During this time, I supervised a number of interpretive events, helped to plan for the fall Fur Trade Encampment, saw the fort's operation continue to run smoothly, and shared additional leadership responsibility with the Acting Superintendent.

SPECIAL ACHIEVEMENT AWARD – 1993

The award was for exemplary accomplishments in the areas of the Resource Management Program, exhibiting rehabilitation program, and the quality living history / visitor services. Also, my personal involvement with the students of Cheraw Middle School in the park, which exemplified my professionalism and true love for the site.

Alejandra, First Lady of the New Bent's Old Fort.

Remembering her time at Bent's Fort.

Bibliography

This book is written mirroring Alejandra's actively working as a Mexican laborer woman in the 20th century using the minimal detailed documentation of a 19th century Mexican laborer woman. The following resources and her own family background were used to develop the character role of Mexican laborer woman at the fort.

Abert, Lieutenant James W., *Western America in 1846-1847; the original travel diary of Lieutenant J. W. Abert, who mapped New Mexico for the United States Army*, John Galvin, Editor, Smithsonian Library.

Galvin, John (Editor), *Through the Country of the Comanche Indians in the Fall of the Year 1846*, Army Corps of Topographical Engineers, J. Howell, San Francisco, CA 1970.

State Historical Society of Colorado, *Bent's Old Fort*, State Historical Society of Colorado, January 1979.

Garrard, Lewis Hector, *Wah-To-Yah and the Taos Trail*, Reprint, Ralph Bieber, ed., Glendale, Calif., 1938.

Grinnell, George Bird, *Bent's Old Fort and its Builders*, Topeka: Kansas State Historical Society, 1923.

Lavender, David, *Bent's Fort*, Doubleday and Company, 1954.

Magoffin, Susan, *Down the Santa Fe Trail and Into Mexico: the Diary of Susan Shelby Magoffin, 1845 – 1847*. Stella Drumm, ed.

Mumey, Nolie. *Old Forts and Trading Posts of the West: Bent's Old Fort and Bent's New Fort on the Arkansas River*, Vol. 1, Denver, Artcraft Press, 1956.

Thompson, Enid, "Life in an Adobe Castle 1833-1849" *Bents Old Fort, Colorado Magazine*, Fall 1977.

Ward Arps, Louisa, "From Tranding Post to Melted Adobe 1849-1920," *Bent's Old Fort, Colorado Magazine*, Fall 1977.

Gwinn W. Heap, *Central Route to the Pacific*, Philadelphia, Penn Lippincott, Grambo, 1854, pp. 24-25.